STOCK CAR Racing

The Thrill of Racing

TOM GREVE

Rourke
Publishing LLC
Vero Beach, Florida 32964

www.rourkepublishing.com

PHOTO CREDITS: © Library of Congress: page 5; ©David Ferroni: page 6; © Graham Bloomfield: page 7; © JACK BRADEN: page 8; © Chrysler Media: page 8; © Bryan Eastham: page 9; © Scott Scheibelhut: page 10; © GM Racing Photo: page 12, 16, 22; © Todd Taulman: page 11, 12, 21; © Eric Gevaeart© Kevin Norris: page 14; © Arlo Abrahamson: page 16; © bsankow: page 17; ©Honda Media: page 18

Edited by Jeanne Sturm

Cover design by Tara Raymo
Interior design by Teri Intzegian

Library of Congress Cataloging-in-Publication Data

Greve, Tom.
  Stock car racing / Tom Greve.
      p. cm. -- (The thrill of racing)
  ISBN 978-1-60472-375-5 (hardcover)
  ISBN 978-1-60472-812-5 (softcover)
  ISBN 978-1-60472-774-6 (ebook)

  1. Stock car racing--United States--History--Juvenile literature. 2. NASCAR (Association)--History--Juvenile literature. I. Title.
  GV1029.9.S74G74 2009

  796.72--dc22

                        2008011251

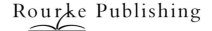

Rourke Publishing

www.rourkepublishing.com – rourke@rourkepublishing.com
Post Office Box 3328. Vero Beach. FL 32964

Table of Contents

Incredible speeds and roaring engines help make stock car racing the most popular motor sport in the United States. Stock car races on television and at the racetracks thrill millions every racing season.

Stock Car Racing Roots

Stock car racing got its start on sand beaches in the early 1900s. After **prohibition** ended, instead of making deliveries, moonshine runners began racing their cars against each other on dirt tracks in the southeastern United States.

Thrilling Fact

Stock Car Racing is the second most popular professional sport in the United States, behind pro football.

NASCAR is Born

In 1948, Bill France Sr. organized the rules of racing and formed NASCAR (National Association of Stock Car Auto Racing) in Daytona, Florida. Since then, the Daytona 500 has become NASCAR's most popular event. Aired in 1979, The Daytona 500 was the first televised NASCAR race.

STOCK CAR RACING
from Beaches to the Big Time

	1900s
1920s	Races on sand beaches
Prohibition era moonshine runs	1930s
1940s	Repeal of prohibition
Races become popular in the Southeast	1948
1979	NASCAR is formed
Daytona 500 becomes first stock car race shown on TV	2008
	NASCAR renames its season the Sprint Cup

NASCAR uses four car models for races: the Chevy Monte Carlo SS, the Toyota Camry, the Ford Fusion, and the Dodge Charger. The body shape of the car looks similar to one you could purchase at a car dealership. The engines in the race cars are modified to produce far more power than a regular car engine.

Cars racing on short tracks and road courses post slower speeds due to more frequent use of the brakes coming into turns.

Different tracks require different car designs. Short-track car designs create **downforce** so they can turn sharply without flipping over. Long-track car designs reduce **drag** for great bursts of speed on **straightaways**. However, NASCAR rules now require **restrictor plates** on long-track cars to prevent drivers from going so fast they lose control.

You Asked...
How fast do stock cars go?
*Cars average 188 **mph** (303 **km/h**) at Talladega Superspeedway.*

NASCAR is a family affair. The Petty and Earnhardt families are two NASCAR dynasties who know triumph as well as tragedy. Richard Petty and Dale Earnhardt Sr. each won seven Championships. Sadly, Earnhardt Sr. died in a crash while racing in 2001, and Richard Petty's grandson Adam died during a practice run in 2000. Both families continue to race.

Richard Petty's nickname is the King.

Dale Earnhardt Sr.'s was the Intimidator.

Drivers like Dale Earnhardt Jr., Jimmie Johnson, Kevin Harvick, and Jeff Gordon are currently the star drivers of the sport. Others, such as Kasey Kahne, Denny Hamlin, and Casey Mears, are rising stars.

Jeff Gordon

Jeff Gordon is from Pittsboro, Indiana. He became the youngest winner in Daytona 500 history in 1997, and he has won four NASCAR championships. He is married and has a daughter named Ella. In 1999, Jeff Gordon founded a charity to help sick children.

After two practice sessions, drivers race in a qualifying time trial to determine which cars and drivers will compete. The driver with the fastest lap time will start in the pole position.

The driver with pole position gets an advantage by being first in line to start the race.

The driver winning the most points in a season is champion. Drivers get 185 points for winning a race

and bonus points for winning laps. After the 26th race, only the top 12 drivers continue in the Chase for the Sprint Cup championship.

The final ten races of the season are NASCAR's playoff to determine a champion.

On race day, NASCAR officials check to make sure every car meets **regulations**. If anything fails to pass inspection, the team can suffer a **disqualification**.

Jimmie Johnson

Jimmie Johnson was born in 1975. He began racing competitively when he was eight. He has won the NASCAR championship two years in a row. He lives in Charlotte, North Carolina, with his wife Chandra.

Big Events

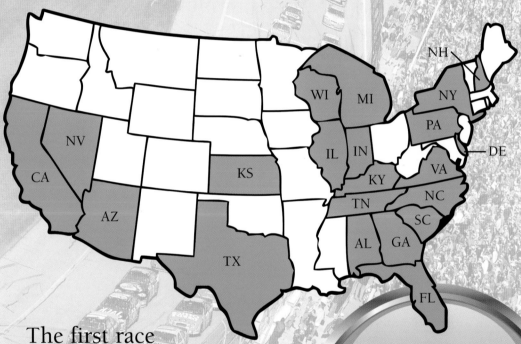

States that host NASCAR Races

NH
WI
MI
NY
PA
DE
NV
IL
IN
CA
KS
KY
VA
AZ
TN
NC
SC
AL
GA
TX
FL

The first race of NASCAR's season is the Daytona 500. The Race is 500 miles (805 km) long, or 200 laps around the track.

Thrilling Fact

Each February, more than 160,000 fans attend the Daytona 500 in person and millions more watch on TV.

Races are held on weekends. Race day starts with NASCAR officials inspecting cars and reviewing the rules with the teams. Drivers cannot get into their cars until five minutes after the singing of the National Anthem.

NASCAR fans are very loyal. Faithful fans, called the NASCAR Nation, travel around in RVs to watch their favorite drivers compete at different races.

Martinsville Speedway, in use since 1948, is also NASCAR's shortest track.

There are 36 NASCAR races a year. Most are on oval-shaped tracks of various lengths. One lap around the Martinsville Speedway in Virginia is only about a half mile (0.8 km) long, but a lap at Talladega Superspeedway is almost 3 miles (4.5 km) around.

Two races are on road courses, which twist and turn in all directions. All tracks are concrete or asphalt.

One of only two NASCAR road races, Watkins Glen's course in New York state is 2.5 miles (4 km) around.

During races, drivers need gas, new tires, or repairs for the race car. When this happens, the driver makes a pit stop. The pit is located directly alongside the racetrack. The pit crew works while the driver remains in the car.

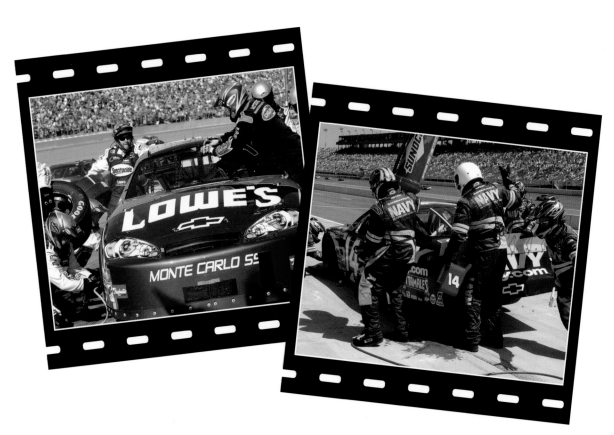

A pit stop for new tires and gas takes just 12 to16 seconds. Longer pit stops hurt a team's chances to win the race.

NASCAR drivers race as part of a team. Teams include drivers, an owner, a **sponsor**, and groups of workers to keep the cars running in top form.

Racing team mechanics work year-round preparing their cars for races.

Stock car racing is a dangerous and sometimes deadly sport. Safety measures, like the head and neck security (HANS) device, protect drivers. NASCAR always works to improve safety without reducing the thrill of the sport.

Wearing a HANS device helps drivers survive crashes by preventing the head and neck from snapping forward or back.

Like most motorsports, NASCAR uses a system of flags to relay safety information to the drivers. During races, different flags indicate different track conditions or events unfolding in the race.

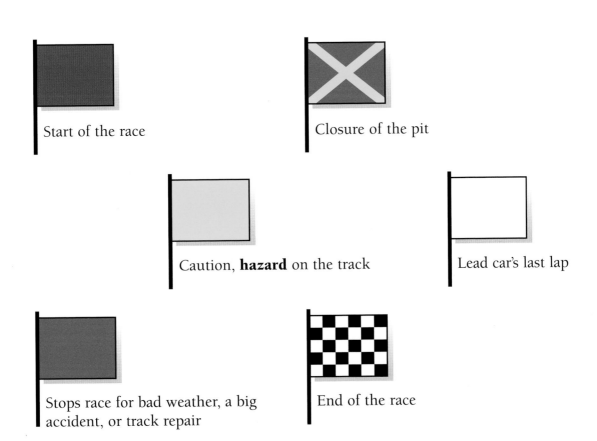

Start of the race

Closure of the pit

Caution, **hazard** on the track

Lead car's last lap

Stops race for bad weather, a big accident, or track repair

End of the race

NASCAR's popularity generates big money, but it costs a lot to compete. Team owners have to pay the pit crew, the driver, and other team members.

Operational Costs

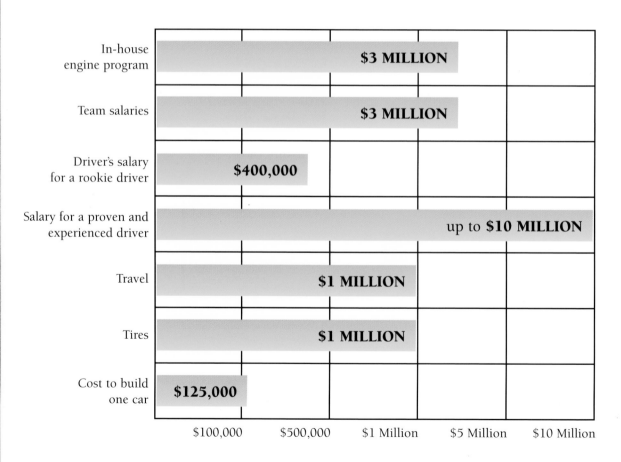

	$100,000	$500,000	$1 Million	$5 Million	$10 Million
In-house engine program			$3 MILLION		
Team salaries			$3 MILLION		
Driver's salary for a rookie driver	$400,000				
Salary for a proven and experienced driver				up to $10 MILLION	
Travel		$1 MILLION			
Tires		$1 MILLION			
Cost to build one car	$125,000				

NOTE: THE GRAPH IS NOT DRAWN TO SCALE.

NASCAR teams rely on sponsors for money. Sponsors are corporations that pay for a team's operational costs in exchange for having their name or logo displayed on the race car. Sponsors pay teams between 10 to 20 million dollars a season.

Sponsors get advertising exposure and can use the driver for promotional purposes.

NASCAR is no longer just a regional sport. It packs heart-pounding elements of power and speed into a thrilling spectacle that keeps millions of loyal fans from coast to coast excited year-round.

Glossary

disqualification (dis-KWAL-if-uh-KAY-shun): kicked out of a race for breaking a rule

downforce (DOWN-fors): the pressure of air passing over a moving car which pushes the car down so it can make tight turns without flipping

drag (DRAG): the amount of resistance created when the air hits the car

hazard (HAZ-erd): something on the track that threatens safety

km/h (KAY-EM-AYCH): abbreviation for kilometers per hour

mph (EM-PEE-AYCH): abbreviation for miles per hour

prohibition (pro-huh-BISH-un): laws which made alcohol illegal in the 1920s

regulations (reg-yoo-LAY-shunz): rules and guidelines each team must follow

restrictor plates (ri-STRIKT-er PLAYTZ): devices put on engines to limit a car's top speed

sponsor (SPAHN-ser): a company that gives money to a racing team in return for advertising on the race car

straightaways (STRAYT-uh-wayz): long stretches of road or track with no curves

Index

Websites to Visit

http://www.lowesracing.com/kids/index.html

http://www.kidzworld.com/quiz/4479-quiz-nascar-trivia-

http://compactiongames.about.com/library/demos/bl_nascar2003_demo.htm

Further Reading

Buckley, James. *Eyewitness NASCAR*. DK Publishing, Inc., 2005.

DuBois, Paul, Swenter, Jennifer, and Zenz, Aaron. *NASCAR ABCs*. Gibbs Smith, 2007.

Eagen, Rachel. *NASCAR*. Crabtree Publishing Company, 2006.

About the Author

Tom Greve lives in Chicago with his wife Meg. They have two children, Madison and William. He enjoys watching and playing sports, and his hobbies include train travel and bicycle riding.